LIFE REWRITTEN

THE UNBREAKABLE SPIRIT

REGINA L. OBY

Copyright © 2025 by Trinity Publishing Company

All rights reserved. No part of this book may be reproduced or transmitted in any form or by any means, electronic or mechanical, including photocopying, recording, or by any information storage and retrieval system, without permission in writing from the author, except for the inclusion of brief quotations in a review.

Published in USA by Trinity Publishing Company

Paperback ISBN: 978-1-964707-82-2

eBook ISBN: 978-1-964707-83-9

Book Cover Design: Paul Nomshan

Layout and Formatting: R. Muhammad

2 Corinthians 4: 8-9 KJV

"We are troubled on every side, yet not distressed; we are perplexed, but not in despair; persecuted, but not forsaken; cast down, but not destroyed."

TABLE OF CONTENTS

A Breast Cancer Survivor 1

Chapter 1: Faith Feels Far Away 3

Chapter 2: Embracing Storms and Emotions 11

Chapter 3: Surrendering Control and Leaning on Faith 19

Chapter 4: Grace in the Battle 27

Chapter 5: Finding Hope in the Dark 37

Chapter 6: Community, Compassion, and Connection 43

Chapter 7: A Shift in this Journey 49

Chapter 8: The Weight of Truth and the Journey Within ... 59

Chapter 9: Living on Purpose 67

Chapter 10: Faith in the Fire 75

A Breast Cancer Survivor

Isaiah 40:31 (NIV)

"But those who hope in the Lord will renew their strength. They will soar on wings like eagles; they will run and not grow weary; they will walk and not faint."

I am a survivor, a storyteller, and a seeker of faith. My life has been shaped by unexpected challenges, the most profound of which was my breast cancer diagnosis. This is a chapter of my life I never anticipated, a battle I never imagined fighting. Yet, through it all, I have come to see my journey not as a series of setbacks but as a path to transformation of renewing my mind and spirit, the rewriting of my story.

Before cancer, my life was on a path like many others of building and cultivating relationships and pursuing new goals in life. Today, I am passionate about sharing my story, not to dwell on the pain, but to celebrate the resilience, hope, and faith that emerged through it all. I am committed to helping others who face their own struggles, reminding them that while we may not choose the storms in our lives, we can choose how we weather them.

I choose to share my story with you because I believe that the hardest seasons can hold the most profound blessings. It's my hope that I can be an encouraging vessel for someone else to fight to live. Whether you are facing your own health battle or supporting a loved one or simply seeking to live with more faith and purpose, I hope my journey brings you encouragement.

Heavenly Father,

As I begin to share this journey, I come before You with an open heart. I surrender my story into Your hands, knowing that each chapter holds purpose even when the path is difficult to see. I pray that the words within these pages may be a testament to Your unfailing love, a reminder that in our darkest moments, you are there beside us, carrying us when we cannot stand. Amen.

For every reader who opens this book, may they find hope, strength, and comfort. Let these words be a gentle light for anyone facing battles of their own. May they feel your presence in the pages, your peace in the pauses, and your strength in the stories that unfold.

CHAPTER 1

FAITH FEELS FAR AWAY

THE DIAGNOSIS

Job 13:15, KJV-

"Though he slays me, yet will I trust in him: but I will maintain mine own ways before him."

In the moments of uncertainty, faith often becomes less about certainty and more about trust, even when we do not feel it. It is like walking through a dark tunnel without knowing where it leads, trusting that there's light at the end. When faith feels far away, it's often during moments of deep struggles or pain. Remember to breathe and relax; it is what I told myself during these moments.

In 2015, my mother passed away, and I didn't grieve in the way people might expect. I didn't cry or outwardly show pain, but deep inside, I felt something shift. The loss was immense, yet I held it in, not fully allowing myself to experience or express the grief in a way others might have anticipated.

When I began to feel sick in 2017, doctors and others initially thought it was grief manifesting physically. They assumed that the emotional weight I hadn't processed was showing up in my body. At first, I doubted it too; maybe they were right; maybe this was just grief coming out in ways I hadn't understood.

But as time went on and my health continued to decline, I knew otherwise. This wasn't grief. The symptoms I was feeling, the pain and exhaustion, were something deeper, something that couldn't be explained by loss. I had a feeling deep inside me that there was more at play, and it wasn't grief.

Despite my best efforts to maintain my health and continue working, the months leading up to the cancer diagnosis were incredibly difficult. I pushed myself to keep going, but my body was telling me something was wrong. After numerous doctor visits and no answers, I was ultimately put on Family Medical Leave of Absence (FMLA) in order to focus on my health and receive the care I needed.

The truth is that I was exhausted. My mind raced with worry, and despite my efforts to appear strong and composed, I felt like I was unraveling on the inside. I could no longer ignore the signs that something was wrong; after sleepless nights, I finally reached the point of scheduling a mammogram as my last resort to finding the issue.

The mammogram was normal, and this left me confused and concerned because I still felt something wasn't right. I had symptoms that suggested otherwise, and while I wanted to feel reassured, the lack of answers only deepened my unease. I couldn't shake the feeling that something was being overlooked, that my instincts were trying to tell me something my test results couldn't explain.

While on FMLA, I decided to rest and relax for the three months away from work, hoping that giving my body time to heal would bring relief. However, the pain and discomfort did not go away, and this was incredibly frustrating. No matter how much I rested or tried to distract myself, the discomfort persisted, as a constant reminder that something was wrong.

The last week of FMLA, on that Friday morning, I was showering when I felt a large lump underneath my right arm. A wave of dread washed over me. I immediately called my doctor, who ordered an emergency mammogram for the following Monday morning. Suddenly, the weekend stretched out before me, each hour filled with anxiety and endless "what ifs." The wait felt unbearable; every moment weighed down with the uncertainty of what might come next. It was as if time slowed, and all I could do was sit in that uncomfortable fear and hope.

On Monday morning, I went in for the mammogram, feeling tense but hoping for reassurance. After the scan was complete, I noticed the technician's expression changed; she looked concerned. "Please leave your gown on for an ultrasound," she said gently. This was something new for me, and my heart started to race. The unexpected shift in procedure felt ominous.

Once the ultrasound was finished, the technician said, "Wait here for the doctor." Her words hung in the air, filling the room with heavy silence. I sat there alone, wrapped in the thin fabric gown, feeling the weight of uncertainty pressing down on me, bracing for whatever news might come next.

The doctor walked into the room, looked at me with a somber expression, and asked, "Are you here alone?" I told her that my older sister was waiting outside, and she immediately called her in so she could tell us both what she had discovered.

"You have breast cancer," she said. My sister gasped, and I could see the shock in her eyes, though for me, it wasn't entirely unexpected. I'd felt for a while that something was wrong, but hearing it confirmed out loud still made everything feel surreal.

What the doctor said next, though, took me by surprise: "We've scheduled an emergency biopsy for tomorrow morning at 7 a.m." The urgency in her words brought a new weight to everything. I wasn't expecting things to move this fast, and suddenly, the reality of it all came crashing down.

I was taken aback by the sudden urgency. My mind raced, grasping to understand just how serious this was. Until now, everything had moved so slowly, weeks of tests, waiting, and wondering. But in that moment, it was like time sped up, the pace shifting from slow to a whirlwind of decisions and appointments.

As we left the office, my sister kept looking at me, searching for words of comfort. But I could tell that, just like me, she was grappling with the enormity of it all, both of us processing in our own way. The world felt heavy and out of focus, and yet there was no turning back.

Now came one of the hardest parts: I had to tell my family. I had to find the words to tell my siblings and my children that this is happening, that

I have breast cancer. Just the thought of it felt like too much to bear. I wanted to protect my children from this news, to shield them from the pain and fear I knew it would bring, but I also knew they needed to hear it from me.

I tried to imagine how each conversation would go. My children—they'd been my support and my closest allies. They would be heartbroken but strong. I knew, trying to take on some of the weight themselves. And then my closet friends and family, telling them, would be different. I have to express the strength I have in order for them to keep it together. I hesitated to tell my children about my cancer diagnosis because they were already carrying the emotional weight of watching their young cousin fight the same disease. I knew this news would add even more stress to their hearts.

In my mind, I kept searching for the right words, but every attempt felt inadequate. How do you tell people you love that your world has changed in an instant? How do you prepare them for a journey you're barely prepared to face yourself? I knew that, somehow, I had to summon the strength to do it. I needed them by my side, and even though I feared their reactions, I knew that together, we would find our way through.

When I finally picked up the phone and began dialing, I took a deep breath, trying to steady myself. It was time to share my burden, to let them in on the battle that was now ours to face as a family.

I gathered my children to tell them, and the look on their faces was bright and carefree, completely unaware of the storm brewing in my heart. I could feel my palms sweating as I sat down, their laughter fading into silence as they sensed something was off. "Can we talk for a minute?" I asked, my voice shaky. They nodded, their expressions shifting from curiosity to concern. I took a deep breath, preparing myself to explain something so complicated in a way they could understand.

I just found out that I have breast cancer. Their faces fell, confusion washing over them. I could see the questions forming in their eyes, and I quickly reassured them, "I'm going to be okay. We're going to get through this together."

But the tears were already spilling down my cheeks as I watched their expressions change from confusion to worry. As I spoke, I could see my children processing the news, their minds grappling with the gravity of it all. I felt their fear, their innocence shattering, and my heart ached for them. But I also felt a sense of determination swell within me. I would fight this battle for them, and together, we would lean on each other, finding strength and love.

After hanging up with my friends and family, I took a moment to collect myself. I knew the days that followed would be filled with a whirlwind of emotions. Their support reminded me that I was not alone in this fight. I also leaned on my children, using this as an opportunity to show them resilience and hope.

Though fear lingered in the background, I could also feel the threads of hope weaving through our conversations. I knew that we would face whatever came next together, and that made all the difference.

The anxiety felt like a constant companion, pulsing through my every thought. I questioned everything: my health, my choices, and the impact of this diagnosis on my loved ones. It was hard to find peace in the midst of such confusion. But as I leaned on God, family, and friends, I understood that the anxiety was a part of the process, not the end of the story. It was a constant reminder that I wasn't alone, even when I felt overwhelmed.

When shadows fall and faith seems thin,
And doubt seeps softly, creeping in,
I whisper prayers, though faint and slow, and seek the strength I use to know.
The journey winds, the valley steep; my heart is worn, my spirit weak.
Yet somewhere in the darkened haze, a quiet voice still calls to praise.
For faith, though tested, bruised, and worn, is like the light before the dawn.
It flickers gently, dim but true, reminding me of what is due.
Not every path is clear and straight, not every answer short to wait, but even when I'm lost, astray, I cling to hope to find the way.
So, though my spirit shakes and bends, this tested faith will stand again.
Through brokenness, my heart will say, I'll trust Him, come what may.

Oby Strong

CHAPTER 2

EMBRACING STORMS AND EMOTIONS

THE RESULTS

Romans 5:3-4 KJV

"And not only so, but we glory in tribulations also: knowing that tribulation worketh patience; and patience, experience; and experience, hope."

After what felt like an eternity of waiting, the day arrived for the result of my biopsy. The atmosphere was heavy with anticipation as I sat in the doctor's office, my heart racing with both hope and fear. I had been through so much in such a short time, and now I was about to get the details of my diagnosis and treatment plan.

When the doctor entered the room, I could see the professionalism in her demeanor, but I also sensed her empathy. She sat across from me, and I could feel the weight of her words hanging in the air. "We received the results from your biopsy," she began, her voice steady but gentle.

She detailed the findings; I hung onto her every word, trying to process the information. The biopsy confirmed that I had HER2 and Stage 3.

March 2018, the mammogram results: A new irregular 3.0 cm mass in the 9:00 right breast is highly suggestive of malignancy and corresponds to the patient's painful palpable area of concern. The dilated duct extends from the mass to the nipple and may represent intraductal extension. An ultrasound-guided biopsy of the 3.0 cm mass in the 9:00 right breast is recommended. Irregular 1.0 cm mass in the 6:00 subareolar right breast at 6 o'clock is suspicious and may represent a satellite mass/intraductal extension. An ultrasound-guided biopsy is recommended. An oval 0.7 cm mass in the right breast at 7 o'clock is suspicious and likely represents a satellite mass. Further management of this mass pending histopathology of the biopsied masses is recommended. There are at least 4 abnormal right axillary lymph nodes. The largest lymph node, measuring 1.8 cm, is highly suggestive of malignancy. An ultrasound-guided biopsy is recommended.

The ultrasound results: Ultrasound demonstrates an irregular vascular solid mass with micro lobulated margins measuring 3.0 x 2.4 x 2.8 cm (about 1.1 in) seen in the right breast at 9 o'clock located 5 centimeters (about half the length of the long edge of a credit card) from the nipple with an associated dilated duct extending to the nipple. These findings are suggestive of intraductal extension. Internal echotexture is hypoechoic.

There is an irregular solid mass with indistinct margins measuring 1.0 x 0.5 x 0.6 cm (about 0.24 in) seen in the 6:00 subareolar right breast.

Internal echotexture is hypoechoic. This may represent an area of intraductal extension/satellite mass. There is an oval mass with indistinct margins measuring 7 x 3 x 5 mm (about 0.2 in) seen in the right breast at 7 o'clock located 5 centimeters (about 1.97 in) from the nipple. Internal echotexture is hypoechoic. This mass represents a satellite mass.

There is an oval 1.5 x 0.3 x 1.5 cm (about 0.59 in) mass with circumscribed margins seen in the 7:00 right breast located 5 cm (about 1.97 in) from the nipple adjacent to the 7 mm (about 0.28 in) mass with indistinct margins. This oval 1.5 cm (about 0.59 in) mass may represent a cluster of cysts. There are at least 4 abnormal right axillary lymph nodes. The largest abnormal right axillary lymph node measures 1.8 x 1.2 x 1.7 cm (about 0.67 in).

The biopsy results are A: Right breast, 9:00 (ultrasound-guided core biopsy): - Invasive ductal carcinoma with lymphoplasmacytic infiltrate, grade 3 (Nottingham scores: 8) - Tumor present in all 4 cores, largest extent 10 mm (about 0.39 in) - No ductal carcinoma in situ (DCIS) or lymph vascular invasion identified. - Prognostic markers ordered on A1, right breast, 6:00, subareolar (ultrasound-guided core biopsy): - Fragments of fibroadenoma. C: Lymph node, right axilla (ultrasound-guided core biopsy): - Metastatic breast carcinoma in 3 of 4 cores, largest extent 9 mm (about 0.35 in).

Hearing the specifics made everything feel very real. My mind raced as I absorbed the information. I was very upset after getting the results, a wave of emotions crashing over me that I hadn't fully anticipated. Deep down I had known something was wrong long before I received the official diagnosis. The nagging pain, the lump I found, it all felt like my body was trying to communicate something urgent, but no one seemed to listen or hear me.

As I sat in the aftermath of that appointment, a profound sense of frustration washed over me. I felt like I had been shouting into a void, trying to make my concerns heard, only to have them dismissed or minimized along the way. The weight of that realization compounded my feelings of anger and sadness. It was as if I had been on this long, solitary journey, desperately seeking answers, and now I was confronted with the reality of a diagnosis that felt both familiar and shocking.

Tears stung my eyes as I reflected on the weeks leading up to this moment. Each doctor's visit, each test, and every time I tried to express my fears felt like an uphill battle. I had tried to advocate for myself, to articulate my worries, but it often felt like I was met with skepticism. Now, standing in the wake of my diagnosis, I couldn't shake the feeling that I had been brushed aside, my instincts dismissed as mere anxiety.

I took a moment to breathe deeply, grounding myself in the present. While I understood that the medical professionals had to make decisions based on their assessments and protocols, I couldn't help but feel a pang of betrayal. My body had been sending signals, and I had felt so alone in my fight to get the help I needed.

As this passed, I channeled that frustration into determination. I vowed that my voice would be heard from here on out. No more waiting for someone else to take charge of my care. I would be my own advocate, making sure my concerns were taken seriously. I would educate myself about my diagnosis, my treatment options, and the resources available to me.

Sharing my diagnosis with others became a turning point. I tell everyone about the struggles I faced leading up to this moment, the feeling of being unheard, and how that had added to my emotional burden. Their reactions are of shock and empathy. The support helped me realize I wasn't alone in this battle.

With renewed resolve, I focused on the future. I would approach my treatment with knowledge that I had a voice, and I would use it. The journey ahead would be difficult, but I felt a growing sense of empowerment. I would not only fight for my health but also ensure that experiences could help others who might feel dismissed or overlooked in their own journeys.

It became clear to me that this experience, while painful, could also be an opportunity for growth and change. I would educate myself, seek out the best care, and advocate for myself fiercely. I was determined to turn my frustration into strength, ready to face whatever challenges lay ahead, armed with the knowledge that my voice mattered.

After learning that I had cancer, the next step was genetic testing. It was a pivotal moment in my journey, as I was hoping for answers but uncertain about what the results might reveal. When the genetic test results came back, they showed that I have a genetic mutation called MSH2-MSH3, which is connected to Lynch Syndrome: a condition I inherited from my biological father.

Suddenly, I felt the weight of this new information on my shoulders. Learning that I had inherited this mutation, that it was part of my DNA, stirred a mix of emotions. It explained so much, but it also left me with a feeling of vulnerability. I couldn't help but wonder if this mutation was something my biological father had struggled with or if other family members might have faced similar battles.

Learning that I had Lynch Syndrome was both overwhelming and eye-opening. It explained so much about my health history, and it felt like a key piece of the puzzle had finally clicked into place. But it also brought with it a new set of challenges and a deeper understanding of how my genetic makeup could affect my health in the future.

The knowledge of having Lynch Syndrome was both a burden and a blessing. It meant I had to be vigilant and proactive about my health, and it also opened the door to a deeper understanding of my body's genetic predispositions. It was a stark reminder that my journey was not about the cancer I was fighting but about the legacy of my genetics and how I could use this knowledge to fight even harder for my health, for my family, and for my future.

When storms arise and skies turn gray,
And winds of doubt begin to sway,
We stand tall in the swirling rain, knowing growth comes through pain.
For every storm that rattles the soul, refines the spirit, and makes it whole.
Through every flash, through every tear, we learn to walk without fear.
The thunder roars, the lightning strikes, but with each trial, strength ignites.
Embrace the storm, the fierce and wild, for through its fury, we are styled.
Like trees that bend but never break, we rise again for our own sake.
The storm will pass, but we remain stronger now for having lain.
In winds that howl and skies that cry, we find the courage to defy.
For in the storm, we learn to soar, and in our hearts, hope rises more.

Oby Strong

CHAPTER 3

SURRENDERING CONTROL AND LEANING ON FAITH

THE DOCTORS

Proverbs 3:5-6, KJV

"Trust in the Lord with all thine heart; and lean not unto thy own understanding. In all thy ways acknowledge him, and he shall direct thy paths."

As I moved further along in my cancer journey, I found myself coping with a complex mix of emotions. I am now spending more time advocating for myself, trying to ensure my concerns are taken seriously, and that the idea of surrendering any kind of control is daunting.

Surrendering control and leaning on faith became essential as I navigated this cancer journey. It wasn't easy to let go of the need to control every aspect of my treatment, but I knew it was necessary for my peace of mind and healing. I had to trust that everything would unfold as it should, even when the path seemed uncertain and the future unknown.

Finding doctors I could trust was a crucial part of this process. I needed a team of professionals who not only understood the complexities of cancer but also shared my values, who would listen, and who would be partners in this journey. I sought a doctor who saw me as more than just a diagnosis, who would take the time to explain every step and every decision. It was important for me to feel heard and to have confidence in the people who would be guiding me through this fight.

I started with a referral from my primary care physician, who provided a list of oncologists known for their expertise. I began researching, reading credentials, areas of specialization, and patient reviews. It felt like an enormous responsibility; choosing the right team that could significantly impact my journey.

The first consultation was with an oncologist who had excellent reviews. As I sat in the waiting room, I felt a wave of calming sense of peace. The employees were extremely happy and compassionate to every patient, and the environment was excellent.

When I finally met her, I was struck by her warmth and compassion. She listened intently as I recounted my journey so far, nodding empathetically and answering my questions with clarity. I felt a sense of relief, knowing I was in capable hands.

After a thorough examination and discussion about my diagnosis, she talked about the genetic testing and the treatment options. I appreciated how she took the time to explain each step and encouraged me to ask questions. I left the appointment feeling empowered, as if I had taken a crucial step forward.

I continued my search, meeting with other specialists, including a breast surgeon and a radiation specialist. Each consultant helped me gather more information and solidify my understanding of the path ahead. I was beginning to piece together a team that felt right for me.

Eventually, I found the right team where I felt confident in a compassionate oncologist, an experienced surgeon, and a supportive navigator who would guide me through the process. Together, they laid out a comprehensive treatment plan tailored to my specific situation, including surgery after chemo, followed by radiation.

With each appointment, I felt more in control. I was no longer just a passive recipient of care; I was an active participant in my treatment journey. The newfound team of professionals gave me strength, and I was determined to face whatever challenges lay ahead, armed with a praying support team.

I had to let go and surrender control to God, trusting that He would guide the hands of the doctors and walk them through every decision. I prayed for their wisdom, for clarity in their actions, and for the strength to face whatever came my way.

There was so much uncertainty, so many unknowns, but in those moments, I had no choice but to lean on my faith and trust in both God and the doctors He had placed in my life.

It was a humbling experience, realizing that I couldn't control every outcome, every step, or even the timing of my healing. But I knew that God was with me every step of the way. I asked Him to keep me alive, to give me the strength to endure the treatments and the challenges, and to help me find peace in the midst of it all. I trusted that He would work through the doctors, through the treatments, and through every moment of this journey.

Surrendering control to the doctors was not only a test of trust but also a test of faith. After being dismissed by so many doctors about my health, it became an overwhelming challenge to put my trust in yet another doctor who was supposed to care for me. My journey had been filled with unanswered questions and ignored concerns, and that left me heartbroken and skeptical about seeking further help.

I had been in the healthcare field for years, and I used to trust doctors with questions and concerns. But this experience shattered that trust and opened my heart in ways I never expected. Now, the struggle lies in the overwhelming process of tests, procedures, and endless lab work, with no real follow-up or guidance. I quickly learned that in order to get the care I needed; I had to advocate for myself. No one would follow up unless I kept pushing. So, I became relentless calling, emailing, and messaging doctors over and over, ensuring that my health didn't fall through the cracks. This experience taught me the importance of being my own advocate and not giving up, no matter how many times I felt dismissed.

Surrendering control wasn't easy, but it became my path to peace. I knew I wasn't walking this road alone; God was with me, carrying me through the hardest days, and I held on to the belief that with faith and trust, I would emerge stronger, no matter the outcome.

Surrendering the control of my life to doctors is one of the most overwhelming and stressful things I've ever had to do. It feels like handing over the power of everything that makes me, to someone I barely know. Trusting a stranger with your life is a level of vulnerability that's hard to describe. To face that kind of fear and uncertainty, you have to be emotionally intact, but truthfully, I wasn't. I felt unprepared and scared, trying to hold on to any sense of control while letting go of so much.

And yet, in the midst of that fear, I was blessed to meet one of the most wonderful, intelligent, and compassionate doctors. She didn't just treat me medically; she saw me as a person. Her confidence, her kindness, and her ability to make me feel like I was in good hands changed everything. She assured me that I would be okay, and even in moments when the outcome wasn't guaranteed, she made me feel like I could believe it.

The same doctor, who had become such a source of comfort and reassurance, eventually retired not long after COVID. She entrusted her patients to another doctor, but for me, this transition unleashed another wave of anxiety. All the fears I had when I first met her came rushing back. It felt like I was starting over, relearning how to trust, reestablishing a connection, and once again surrendering my health and life into the hands of someone I didn't know. Just when I had finally found peace and comfort with one doctor, I was faced with the challenge of doing it all over again.

It's a cycle that feels exhausting at times, a constant need to adjust, to let go, and to trust again. Life has a way of throwing curveballs, and as I like to say, life is living, and it keeps on changing. Just when you think you've reached a place of calm, another wave hits, reminding you how unpredictable it all can be.

But even in the midst of the chaos, I thank God for life. Because as hard as it is, it's still a gift. Every transition, every challenge, and every moment of discomfort is an opportunity to grow, to lean into my faith, and to recognize that while people and circumstances may change, God's presence and faithfulness never do.

Sometimes, it's not just the medicine that helps us heal; it's the people who carry us through the process. Her presence reminded me that even when I'm handing over control, God is still working through others to provide care, comfort, and reassurance. It's a hard surrender, but it's also a lesson in trust, both in those we rely on and in God, who places them in our lives.

I've tried to hold the reins so tight,
To chart my course and guide the fight.
But with each step, I lose my way;
I feel the weight of yesterday.
I clench my fists, afraid to fall,
Uncertain in my heart, I call.
But in the silence, I hear Him near.
A whisper soft, a voice sincere.
"Let go, my child, and trust in Me;
Release your grip, and you will see.
The path you seek, the peace you crave,
Is found when you, your soul, will save.
So now I breathe; I close my eyes.
And lift my fear to endless skies,
I surrender all, and in the fall,
I trust that God will catch it all.
No longer do I strive alone;
In His embrace, my heart has grown.
For in His hands, my trust will stay,
As faith and grace will light up the way.

Oby Strong

Chapter 4

Grace in the Battle

Treatments

2 Corinthians 12:9, KJV

"And he said unto me, my grace is sufficient for thee: for my strength is made perfect in weakness. Most gladly therefore will I rather glory in my infirmities, that the power of Christ may rest upon me."

Two weeks before my treatment was set to begin, I was admitted to day surgery to have a port placed. The port would be used for administering medications and treatments easily.

The procedure itself was straightforward. Full of emotions, it felt like another step into the unknown. It was a reminder that this journey wasn't going to be easy, that I had just begun the fight for my healing. I wasn't just surrendering to the treatment; I was preparing myself for battle, arming myself with the strength, faith, and resilience that had carried me so far.

As I prepared to start my first round of chemotherapy, a swirl of emotions engulfed me. The determination to fight was again creating anxiety. I promised myself to embark upon this journey with a smile every day and a sense of joy. The journey that had led me to this moment had been filled with uncertainty, and now I was about to embark on a new phase of my battle against cancer.

The treatments for breast cancer are varied and depend on the type, stage, and specific characteristics of the cancer. After my diagnosis, I began a treatment journey that was both physically and emotionally challenging.

The chemotherapy treatments were grueling, with side effects that left me feeling exhausted, weak, and at times emotionally drained. But with every round, I knew that I was one step closer to fighting this disease. I had to dig deep within myself to find strength during the days when I couldn't recognize my own reflection in the mirror, when my hair fell out, when my body seemed to be failing me. I had to trust that the treatment was working, even when it felt like I was losing parts of myself.

After several rounds of chemotherapy (Docetaxel, Herceptin, and Carboplatin), something felt terribly wrong. I was admitted to the hospital due to the chemo drugs causing my heart to fail, leading to congestive heart failure. This unexpected turn in my treatment was terrifying. It felt like everything I had been fighting for was slipping away, and I was being told I could no longer continue with chemo.

The news from my oncologist hit me like a punch to the gut. I was already exhausted from the physical toll of the treatments, but to hear that chemo had to be stopped when I wasn't even halfway through the process was devastating. I felt like I had failed somehow, and in that moment, I felt a deep sense of fear and hopelessness. Without being able to complete the full course of chemo, without ringing that bell as a sign of finishing, I questioned if I would make it through.

It wasn't just the physical setback; it was the emotional blow that shook my spirit. I had been so focused on the goal of completing treatment, of finishing strong, and now I was confronted with the reality that things weren't going as planned. The uncertainty was overwhelming. Would I die because I couldn't finish the treatment? Was there hope for me without the full chemo regimen?

It was one of the darkest moments of my journey. But even then, I had to remind myself that my fight wasn't over. Though I couldn't finish the treatment as I had envisioned, I wasn't defeated. My journey wasn't defined by a bell or by a protocol that didn't work. I had to find a new strength and, even in the uncertainty, trust that God had a different plan for me, a plan that would lead to healing, whether or not it fit the typical mold.

After failed chemotherapy and the diagnosis of heart failure, my next step was thirty-three consistent days of radiation. I knew it was another tough chapter in my journey, but I also knew it was necessary to fight this cancer with everything I had left. Radiation was meant to target any remaining cancer cells, but it came with its own set of challenges and side effects that were hard to bear.

As the days of radiation went on, my skin began to react. It became inflamed, irritated, and painful. I remember the skin starting to peel and even oozing blood, a stark reminder of the toll the treatments were taking on my body. It's unsettling to see my skin change so drastically, to feel the pulse of discomfort with every touch. The pain was constant, and it was hard to keep pushing through; every day seemed to bring new challenges.

But in the midst of the physical pain and the frustration of not knowing how much longer I could endure, I found my faith and resilience tested in ways I had never imagined. Each session of radiation felt like a battle, but I knew I had to keep going. I had come this far through so many rounds of treatments, setbacks, and hospital visits, and I couldn't give up now.

Despite the physical toll, I tried to hold on to the hope that the radiation was doing its job. I had to trust that the pain, the discomfort, and the changes to my body would lead to healing. I focused on the small victories, the moments when I felt stronger, when I made it through a treatment without breaking down. Even in my weakest moments, I knew that each day of radiation brought me closer to the end of this fight, and I had to keep pushing through.

Months after completing radiation and healing, it was finally time for my double mastectomy. I had been through so much already; this was another part of the journey. My surgeon was incredible, compassionate, skilled, and patient. I felt reassured that I was in good hands, even as the reality of surgery loomed over me.

There would be a double mastectomy, lasting a grueling 14 hours. It felt like an eternity, knowing that my body was about to undergo such a profound transformation. Not only was it a double mastectomy, but it also included a lymphadenectomy, where they removed the lymph nodes on my right side. This surgery wasn't just about removing cancer; it felt like I was losing a part of myself, a part that I long associated with my identity as a woman.

The second part of the surgery was for expander placement, part of the reconstruction process. The expanders would gradually stretch the tissue to prepare for future reconstruction, helping to restore the shape of my chest. This was a bittersweet moment; while I was grateful for the medical advancements that would help restore some sense of normalcy, I couldn't ignore the emotional weight of what was happening. My body was changing in many ways I hadn't imagined, and the physical pain of it all would be intense. Yet, I focused on the purpose behind it: the fight to rid my body of cancer and to ensure a better future.

When I woke up after the fourteen-hour surgery, I was in a haze, groggy from anesthesia and feeling the weight of everything I had just gone through. The pain was sharp, and I could feel the changes in my body, but there was a sense of relief as well. I had made it through another part of the journey. The surgeons had done their work, and I was one step closer to healing, one step closer to being cancer-free.

Months before I could proceed with the planned reconstruction surgery, complications arose, the expanders, meant to prepare my body for the next stage, became infected. This was a devastating setback, one that felt like yet another cruel twist in an already challenging journey. I had been mentally preparing myself for the reconstruction, for the sense of restoration that it symbolized, but now that hope was delayed indefinitely.

The infection meant that the expanders had to be removed, and I found myself back at square one, faced with a new reality and the need to adopt a different plan. This setback was more than just physical; it was deeply emotional, a reminder of how unpredictable and relentless this journey could be. Every time I thought I was making progress, something seemed to pull me back.

I had to adjust my expectations to let go of the vision I had of what reconstruction would look like and when it would happen. I reminded myself that healing isn't always a straight line. Sometimes it requires detours, and sometimes it demands more patience than I ever thought I had. With faith, I knew I had to trust the process, even when it veered off course, and believe that there was still a way forward, even if it was different from what I had originally envisioned.

Later on, my oncology surgeon, seeing the challenges I faced with expanders, consulted with a specialized doctor to devise a new approach. The next doctor, a skilled plastic surgeon, carefully reviewed my case and discussed options that might give me a more stable and long-lasting outcome. He recommended an alternative to expanders and implants, the DIEP flap (Deep Inferior Epigastric Perforator) procedure.

In this procedure, instead of relying on implants, he would reconstruct my breast using tissue and muscle from my abdomen. It was a complex and lengthy surgery, but it had significant advantages. By using my own tissue, the risk of infection would be much lower, and the results would feel more natural and more resilient in the long term. This approach seemed like the best plan, and after everything I'd been through, I wanted to choose the best chance for lasting healing.

It was a lot to take in, knowing that this new plan involved another major surgery and a long recovery. But for the first time in a while, I felt hopeful about the path forward. This plan not only addressed my medical needs but also offered a sense of wholeness, of reclaiming what cancer had tried to take from me. I knew the road ahead would be tough, but with this new plan, I was ready to keep pushing forward toward healing and renewal.

About a month after the surgery, I noticed significant swelling in my left arm. It was enormous, and I had no idea what was happening. Alarmed and unsure, I was admitted back into the cancer hospital. After several tests, the doctors told me that I had developed a blood clot in my left arm. Along with the clot, there came severe swelling, and I was diagnosed with lymphedema in that arm.

I was confused and frustrated. How could this happen in my left arm when the lymph nodes had been removed from my right side? The doctors patiently explained that when lymph nodes are removed, the fluid in the body has to find an alternate path, and this disruption can cause complications like lymphedema.

Now, on top of everything else, I was placed on blood thinners and had to adjust to managing this new condition. It felt like one more hurdle in an already overwhelming journey. I didn't understand it all at the time, but I began to see this yet another chapter of the story I was living and journaling, a story of perseverance, faith, and learning to adapt to whatever challenges came my way.

After this diagnosis, my oncologist informed me that I would need to see yet another specialist, a hematologist. It felt overwhelming to add another doctor to the growing list of people I had to trust with my care. Reluctantly, I surrendered to this process, knowing it was necessary for my survival.

After my initial visit, lab tests revealed that my clotting numbers were dangerously high, indicating that my body was still forming clots. The hematologist explained that I would need to be on blood thinners for the rest of my life. I tried to process this new reality, but the fear was undeniable. Blood clots had already claimed the lives of people I cared about, and now this invisible threat was inside my own body.

Later, I developed another blood clot, adding to my fears. The process of clotting became a terrifying ordeal, and it was a constant reminder of how fragile life can be. But even in the face of this frightening reality, I chose to push through. I couldn't let fear define my journey. Each day, I reminded myself that my faith and determination were stronger than the challenges I faced.

This experience taught me to hold on to hope, even when the plan changes. The journey might look different now, but I was still moving forward, one step at a time, embracing the strength I had developed along the way.

In the fiercest storm, when hope feels lost,
When faith is tested, no matter the cost.
Grace whispers softly, a calming refrain,
Strength for the weary, peace in the pain.
The battle rages, but you stand tall,
Not by your might, but by grace, after all.
In every trial, in every tear,
Grace walks beside you, casting out fear.
Through the fiercest fight, when all seems dim,
God's grace will carry you, lifting you within.
In moments of weakness, His power is shown;
Grace makes you stronger than you've ever known.
So, hold to His promise, embrace His call,
For grace is the anchor, the shield, and the wall.
In the midst of the battle, remember this truth:
Grace will see you through, from the old to the new.

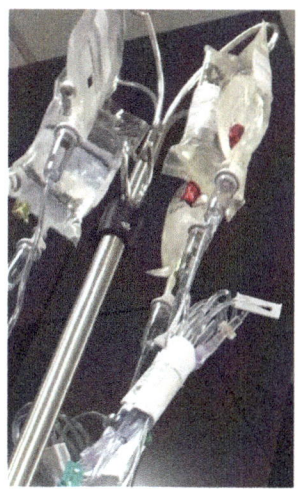

Oby Strong

CHAPTER 5

FINDING HOPE IN THE DARK

COVID

After everything I'd already endured, COVID hit, bringing with it a whole new layer of isolation and fear. As a cancer patient with a compromised immune system, I was already accustomed to being cautious, but the pandemic intensified everything. Suddenly, I was completely isolated, with even simple trips to the doctor becoming risky and uncertain.

The pain from the surgeries and treatments lingered, and without regular checkups, I felt a constant gnawing anxiety about my health. Each day became a test of patience and resilience, with the loneliness pressing down on me. Not being able to see my doctors regularly left me feeling as though I was cut off from essential lifelines, and that added to my growing sense of vulnerability.

I clung to my faith and tried to stay strong, but there were moments when the isolation felt overwhelming. It wasn't just the physical pain I was dealing with, but it was also the mental and emotional weight of carrying on without the support and presence of the people who had been helping me through every step. I found myself needing to dig deeper, to find comfort and strength in the smallest of things, and to believe that somehow, I could get through this, too.

During COVID, I found myself facing yet another challenge. I came down with a fever and became very sick at home. Under normal circumstances, I would have reached out for help, maybe called my doctor, or gone to the emergency room. But with the world in lockdown, everything was closed, including pharmacies and doctors' offices. I was left to navigate this on my own.

I remember feeling an overwhelming sense of fear, even about calling 9-1-1. The thought of going to the hospital, with my immune system already compromised, terrified me.

I was more afraid of what could happen if I were exposed to COVID in the hospital than of the illness I was facing alone at home. So, I did the only thing I could, I prayed for strength, for guidance, for healing, and for the courage to get through this moment.

Living alone, I had no one physically there to lean on. I had to figure out how to care for myself, how to manage the fever, and how to push through the fear. I used every bit of knowledge and strength I had, reminding myself that I had already survived so much and that I wasn't truly alone, even if it felt that way. My faith became my anchor in those moments, helping me find peace amid the isolation and fear.

Never contracting COVID felt like a true blessing amid all the chaos and fear. It was a reminder of God's protection, even in the most isolating and challenging of times. As difficult as those months were, there was a silver lining that came out of it. COVID taught me to lean into my faith even more deeply, to trust God not just when things were manageable but especially when they felt impossible.

A month later, although the fever had finally broken, a new struggle emerged. I found myself unable to eat or drink without getting sick, and everything I tried to keep down wouldn't stay. I was losing weight rapidly, becoming weaker by the day. It was as if my body was reaching its breaking point, and I knew I couldn't continue this way.

My daughter, seeing the urgency, came over to help, wearing a mask and taking every precaution to protect both of us. She called my doctor, and thankfully, they scheduled an emergency visit. When I arrived, a COVID test was immediately performed, after which it didn't take long for them to see the seriousness of my condition, and I was immediately admitted to the hospital. It was a moment of both relief and fear, realizing that things were beyond what I could handle alone.

In the hospital, I felt a wave of gratitude for my daughter's love and vigilance, for her taking charge when I needed it most. This experience was yet another reminder of the importance of the people around me and the strength it takes to allow myself to lean on them when I need it most.

I found strength in knowing that, despite everything, I was watched over and protected. This experience reinforced the power of faith and the importance of surrendering my fears. It showed me that, even when I felt most alone, I was never truly alone; I was never by myself. There was divine presence guiding me, and that assurance helped me grow in gratitude, resilience, and trust.

Psalm 27:1 KJV

"The Lord is my light and my salvation; whom shall I fear? The Lord is the strength of my life; of whom shall I be afraid?"

Holding on to faith, even when things seem dark, is a powerful strength.

Be encouraged and keep moving forward.
When darkness comes and shadows grow,
When strength feels faint and light runs low,
Remember still, the dawn will break,
And hope, though small, begins to wake.
Through silent fears, through endless night,
A spark of faith ignites a light.
It whispers softly, "Just one more day,"
Guiding hearts that lose their way.
Though unseen hands may weave our fate,
Hope waits with us, though time feels late.
In every tear, a chance to heal;
In every ache, strength is arevealed.
So, let the night be what it will,
For hope, like stars, shines brighter still.

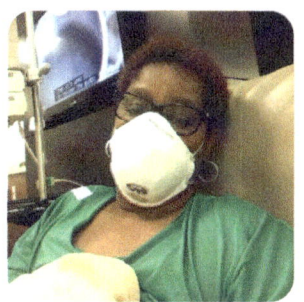

Oby Strong

Chapter 6

Community, Compassion, and Connection

Metaverse & Facebook

During the toughest moments of my sickness, when I was isolated and alone, I found an unexpected lifeline: the Oculus and the metaverse. In this virtual world, I discovered Hardy World Spades, a place where people from all over the world, from all walks of life, came together. What started as a simple game became a powerful source of connection and healing. I met compassionate people who became friends, who understood the need for companionship and laughter during difficult times. Through them, I rediscovered joy, and it felt like a part of my spirit was restored.

Learning to play spades with my grandmother and later with my siblings and family had always been a cherished tradition, and finding a way to reconnect with that part of my life was a blessing. In the metaverse, I was able to laugh, connect, and be a part of something that reminded me of home. This community became more than just people in a virtual space; they became a source of comfort, reminding me that I am never truly alone.

Special thanks to Seeka (Cynthia), Jazzy (Pam), and Jojo (Joelle) for going above and beyond, traveling from other states to support in honor of Breast Cancer Awareness Month. Your kindness, support, and willingness to be there with me in person mean the world. Thank you for showing up, for standing by my side, and for bringing your compassion and love into this journey. I am so grateful for each of you.

Thank you to everyone in Hardy World Spades and the metaverse community for being there, for bringing light and laughter back into my life, and for helping me find strength in the most unexpected places. Thank you for your support.

A special thank you to Hardy West, the visionary creator behind Hardy World Spades. You built more than just a virtual space, you created a sanctuary, a place where we could find peace, drama, laughter, rediscover joy, and share great stories. Through creativity, you gave us a true community, a gathering place to support one another and forge meaningful connections that go beyond the virtual world.

Hardy West, I am deeply grateful for the compassion and dedication you poured into creating this world. You have touched countless lives, including mine, and given us all a place to belong.

I appreciate you for your incredible work, for the joy you've sparked, and for bringing us all together. Thank you for the gift of community and connection.

I used my Facebook platform as a way to reach others, to share my love, and to encourage those who needed it most. Even though my story seems horrific at times, I always reminded myself that there are people out there facing even more difficult battles than mine. It was okay to uplift others, to show love, and to help them see that they were not alone in their struggles.

Each day, I made it a point to encourage others to keep going, to hold on, and to never give up. Life isn't always easy, but through faith and strength, we can, and we will endure. I shared my journey, not for sympathy, but to show that even in the toughest of times, we can find hope, strength, and healing. I created boundaries to protect my peace but used my platform to spread positivity, love, and encouragement.

Sharing my diagnosis on Facebook brought me moments of relief. It reminded me that I wasn't alone. I saw others facing different battles, and I could feel their pain and understand their struggles. It made them my extended family, my Facebook family. As I witnessed others grieving the loss of loved ones to cancer, I was reminded of the gift of life. It made me say, "Thank you, God, for keeping me here." Watching people suffer and fight alongside their families on Facebook inspired me to share my own story. I wanted them to know that they were not alone in their journey. We can get through this together. Love your family, love your friends, and love those who need you during this difficult time. There is a greater need for compassion, and I saw that through the support we share on Facebook. Lord, I thank you for the strength to continue.

Many people would inbox me through Facebook Messenger, telling me I was sharing too much of my life. They said I was too open, too vulnerable.

But God had another plan. I had to learn to shut out the noise, silence the opinions of others, and listen to His voice.

Somewhere in the Facebook world, someone needed support. Someone needed encouragement. And so, I kept going. Even when it felt like I was exposing too much of myself, God reminded me, "Do it for Me." We often say, "Lord, use me," but then we try to put limits on what that means. We want to stay in our comfort zones, speaking only to certain people, going only to certain places, and sharing only what feels safe. But God isn't a limited God. He moves beyond our boundaries, working through every hurt, every pain, and every testimony, no matter the audience or the circumstance.

While sharing my journey on Facebook, I received a message that changed my life. A mother reached out, telling me about her young daughter who was journaling her own battle with childhood cancer. The young lady wanted to meet me, and I was beyond excited.

The day we met was nothing short of life-changing, a moment etched in my heart forever. She had a radiant smile that could light up any room, a smile that carried strength, hope, and wisdom beyond her years. She looked me in the eyes and said, "Never give up. This journey will pass." We hugged tightly and exchanged numbers, promising to stay in touch. True to her words, she called me often, checking on me and encouraging me when I felt weak. One evening, my phone rang, and on the other end was her voice, fragile, crying, and in pain. She was sitting in her closet, fighting through unbearable agony. It was in that moment, hearing her struggles, that I realized she was still fighting for her own life.

Her fight ended shortly after her high school graduation, and my heart felt a weight I couldn't carry. God knew what I needed, and He sent her into my life to teach me something profound: to never lose sight of the beauty in this journey. Her smile remains with me, a constant source of inspiration and a reminder to keep going.

A year before her passing, my children's young cousin also lost her battle to this horrible disease. My mind was consumed with 'why' and questions that seemed to have no answers. The sadness was overwhelming, and I struggled to find meaning. But through these losses, I've learned to carry their light forward, their strength, their smiles, and their courage, they lived on in me. I fight for them, for their memory, and for all those still in the battle. And even in my heaviest moments, I know their spirits are cheering me on.

To this day, I hold their words and actions close to my heart. I think about how, even in their own pain, they chose to love, support, and encourage me. They taught me that even in moments of great sorrow, there's always room for kindness, for connection, and for strength. When I feel weary, I remember her sitting in that closet, crying but still calling me for comfort. I remember her beautiful smile, a smile that defied her pain and radiated hope. And I remember the cousin who was so full of life, taken too soon.

These memories remind me that while the battle is grueling, I am not alone. I am surrounded by angels. God, in His divine timing, showed me the importance of sharing my journey, no matter how vulnerable it makes me feel. He reminded me that my story isn't just for me; it's for others who are still fighting, for those who feel alone, and for those who need a glimmer of hope in their darkest moments. Through these experiences, I've come to understand the power of human connection and the beauty of God's love, even in the midst of pain.

Stay rooted in your journey and always keep God at the center. Don't let others define the story that God has uniquely written for you. Be true to who you are, stand firm in your faith, and continue fighting with courage and purpose. God bless you abundantly.

We gather here, a circle wide,
Bound by compassion, side by side.
In a shared embrace, our spirits rise,
Lifting each other to brighter skies.
Through trials faced and burdens shared,
We find a love that's deeply cared for.
A handheld tight, a gentle word,
In quiet strength, our hearts are stirred.
Each heart a thread, each voice a part,
Together woven, soul to heart.
In kindness sown, we plant and grow a vast garden where blessings flow.
So, here we stand, though paths may roam, in this embrace, we all find home.
In unity, our spirits blend, a family forged, friend by friend.

Oby Strong

Chapter 7

A Shift in this Journey

A New Diagnosis

Isaiah 43:19, KJV

"Behold, I will do a new thing; now it shall spring forth; shall ye not know it? I will even make a way in the wilderness, and rivers in the desert."

A major shift came in my journey just when I thought cancer was behind me. I was finally in the healing process, trying to regain my strength, when my body took a turn that I wasn't prepared for. One day, I went for a walk but couldn't make it back home. I had to call a friend to pick me up and get me back home safely. Over the following days, I found myself reaching out to that same friend again, until eventually I had to call for a ride to the emergency room. By then, my speech was slurred, and my body was failing me in ways I couldn't understand. The doctors initially thought it was a stroke, and they ran a full workup, only to rule it out.

The hospital stay that followed was a whirlwind of confusion, fear, and tests. They couldn't pinpoint the cause of the slurred speech and loss of balance. Eventually, after a lumbar puncture, I was diagnosed with GAD65 (Glutamic Acid Decarboxylase 65), which is an enzyme involved in producing gamma-aminobutyric acid, a key neurotransmitter that helps regulate nerve activity in the brain and nervous system. When the immune system mistakenly attacks GAD65, it can lead to neurological and autoimmune disorders. Just as I was processing this, another diagnosis of Stiff Person Syndrome was given. This syndrome is a rare neurological disorder that affects the central and nervous system, leading to severe muscle stiffness and painful spasms. It is believed to be an autoimmune condition, often associated with GAD65. Later I was diagnosed with Hereditary Ataxia (neurological disorders that cause a loss of balance), Cerebellar Ataxia with Progressive Multifocal Leukoencephalopathy (PML), a life-altering condition. Living with PML has changed everything; I face difficulties walking and speaking. I often feel overwhelmed by the emotional toll of these ongoing challenges.

This year, I spent my birthday and the Fourth of July holiday in the hospital, receiving treatment after treatment, from steroids, plasma, and IVIG, all without success. The next step was Rituximab, a treatment I may need for life. Each new diagnosis and every new test seem to reveal yet another piece of this painful puzzle, a reminder that life is not the same.

Recently, a positive Intrinsic Factor Blocking AB, Parietal Cell AB, and Autoimmune Gastritis result added yet another layer to this journey. The toll on my mental health is enormous, with each day bringing new worries and tests. But even as I struggle, I remind myself that I'm still here, holding on and finding strength in whatever I can. This journey is filled with unknowns, but I'm trying to face them with the courage I have left.

After spending three months in the hospital, I developed a blood clot in my jugular vein. It was one of the scariest moments of my journey. I had gone from dealing with clots in my arms to facing this life-threatening complication. To make matters worse, my left arm, the only arm available for use, was already affected by lymphedema.

The constant poking, prodding, and IV insertions took their toll. Eventually, my left arm was no longer viable for IVs, so they moved to my feet. That, too, was short-lived, as the IVs repeatedly blew due to the steroids being administered. With no other options, the medical team attempted to place an IV in my neck. They avoided the left side initially because of the clot in my jugular, opting for the right side instead. After a week, the IV site on the right side of my neck became infected and had to be surgically removed.

Following a week of waiting and further testing, they determined the clot in my left jugular vein had resolved, and an IV was placed on the left side of my neck. Despite this, I lived in constant fear, a fear that the IV would fail, that another infection would develop, or that I wouldn't make it through this ordeal.

Over the next two and a half months, I endured relentless treatments: 10-15 rounds of plasma exchange and multiple attempts to stabilize my health. The plasma treatments caused more complications, and I was coded several times during my hospital stay. It was one of the darkest and most challenging times of my life.

When the plasma exchange failed, the doctors turned to IVIG (Intravenous), but that, too, didn't work. The next step was Rituximab, an immunotherapy/chemotherapy drug used for various conditions. I was told that this treatment might be lifelong, though nothing was certain.

As if the physical challenges weren't enough, navigating the healthcare system added another layer of stress. My primary care physician suggested I see specialists at the Mayo Clinic, but my insurance didn't cover the doctors I needed most. The weight of this news crushed me, physically, mentally, and emotionally.

Even now, as I write this, tears stream down my face. The healthcare system, one meant to provide hope and healing, feels broken. This experience has been more than just a battle with my body; it has also been a battle with a system that often leaves people like me feeling overlooked and unsupported. Despite it all, I'm holding on, trusting God, and finding strength in the smallest victories. But the journey is far from over.

The falls have become a relentless part of my daily life, each one taking a toll on my body and spirit. One fall left me with a fractured foot, another with a bruised forehead, and many with aches that last for longer than the bruises. It's a lot to process and understand why this is happening to me, but during difficult moments, I hold onto the belief that God hasn't left my side.

For years, I lived under the belief that I had suffered a stroke or a TIA. Doctors pointed to my symptoms that mirrored those of a stroke, but they could never pinpoint the evidence to confirm it. The uncertainty lingered, leaving me without clear answers.

Now, after years of questions and misdiagnoses, I finally have clarity. It wasn't a stroke; it was hereditary ataxia all along. This revelation brings a bittersweet relief. On one hand, it's hard to reconcile the years of misunderstanding. On the other hand, knowing the truth allows me to better understand my body and take the steps I need to move forward.

What keeps me going is my need for independence, to still have some control over my life. I can see the frustration in those around me they worry, they want to help more, but I need to do what I can on my own. This independence isn't just about being able to move freely; it's a lifeline for my mental health, a way to still feel strong and capable despite everything that's happening. My journey is one of perseverance and faith, holding tight to my independence as best I can.

Hearing the doctors link all of this back to cancer, likely from Lynch Syndrome, has been a difficult reality to process. It's as if I'm constantly uncovering new layers to this battle, each one more challenging than the last. Recently, I had a PET scan, another step in this journey, making me feel that even as I fight for my health, I'm also fighting to hold onto hope and resilience.

Adding the possibility of stomach cancer to the list along with Lynch Syndrome, GAD-65, Stiff Person Syndrome, and PML is overwhelming, exhausting, and at times, just plain unfair. Every new diagnosis, every setback, feels like an additional weight on my shoulders. I'm fighting this thing called life, pushing forward despite the frustration, despite the pain, and holding tight to whatever strength I have left. The uncertainty is daunting, but I refuse to let it define my spirit. I'm here, taking it one day at a time, focused on winning this fight for myself and for the hope that continues to light my path.

Eating, something I once took for granted, has now turned into a daily battle. Keeping my weight up feels like an impossible challenge, and walking has become a journey in itself, each step laced with fear that I might fall. I've started using a wheelchair in the house occasionally, but

I'm stubborn I want to walk, so I push myself, step after shaky step, refusing to let go of that independence.

Now, I'm told my body isn't absorbing vitamin B12, no matter how much I take. This lack of nutrients, combined with everything else PML, Lynch Syndrome, and cancer is overwhelming. It's hard knowing that my immune system, which should protect me, seems to be struggling, and I find myself laughing at the irony sometimes. I've joked with friends, "Why couldn't my parents leave me a puppy or a house instead of a genetic disorder?" There's humor in that thought, but underneath, there's a quiet sadness. Somehow, I know that God must have chosen me to bear this burden for a reason, perhaps because He believes I have the strength to endure. And through it all, I say, Thank you, Lord.

Learning later that the medication and all the steroids were causing my blood sugar to spike was yet another weight to carry. Another layer to my health journey. Bringing more anxiety and adding to the strain on my mind and body. Just when I felt I had a handle on things, these new challenges emerged. Still, I am determined to keep pushing forward, holding onto faith as I navigate each added hurdle.

Now, with insulin added to the regimen, I'm learning to give myself B12 shots, and I'm managing a total of thirty-six pills daily, each carrying its own set of side effects. It's a heavy load to bear, both physically and emotionally. This journey has been unrelenting, each new treatment testing my resolve, but I'm committed to pressing on, no matter how taxing. Holding onto hope, I keep moving forward, one day at a time.

It's a profound shift, going from a life that felt whole, full of work and routine, to an uncharted world shaped by loss, pain, and profound changes in every part of who you are. Losing your mom, enduring constant pain, and now facing a journey that reshapes your physical, emotional, and spiritual self in ways you could have never imagined. It's an overwhelming transformation, one that challenges every part of you yet calls for resilience you never knew was there. Through each struggle, you find new depths of strength and faith, redefining what it means to live, to love, and to hope.

Due to Lynch syndrome, I need to have colonoscopies every one to three years. Most of these colonoscopies reveal a few polyps, which are often precancerous. However, this year was different. Along with a colonoscopy, I underwent an esophagogastroduodenoscopy (EGD); a doctor looks at the lining of your esophagus, stomach, and duodenum. After the biopsies, my doctor requested additional labs. Before proceeding, I prayed constantly, asking God to guide me through whatever the outcome might be. When the results came back, they were positive for a condition called antralized, atrophic gastric mucosa with lymphoplasmacytic infiltrates in the lamina propria and intestinal metaplasia. The overwhelming breakdown of this diagnosis: Antralized: The changes in the antrum, the lower part of the stomach, are responsible for a hormone that stimulates stomach acid.

Atrophic gastric mucosa: the lining of my stomach is thinned and weakened of its normal glandular structures. Lymphoplasmacytic infiltrates in lamina propria: A critical presence of lymphocytes and plasma cells, white blood cells, within the lamina propria. Intestinal metaplasia: the existence of intestinal cells within the stomach lining, which is a precancerous change and marker for the growth risk of gastric cancer.

I have no idea what most of this means, and it's another scary moment I have to face. To make matters worse, the new gastric specialists are leaving me with the same frustration I've felt before, that no one seems to truly listen. The most overwhelming part of this journey is the feeling of not being heard, even when I know I'm sick. It's exhausting, both physically and emotionally. Stress and worry often consume the calmness and clarity I try to maintain in my life.

Lately, I've been burdened with a constant fear that I may already have gastric cancer. Every day, I'm reminded that I've inherited a serious illness from one of my biological parents, and it weighs on me. I know my body is different from most. People often tell me to eat certain foods, drink this, or avoid that, as if these things could prevent or cure my condition. What they don't know is that my body, my makeup, and my genetic pool are entirely different from theirs. Some of the foods they suggest, such as certain vegetables, don't heal me; instead, they make me sicker.

This isn't just about cancer. I'm living with an inherited disease that affects not only my stomach but also my brain and entire body. It's a daily battle that most people can't comprehend. In my heart, I believe that the only cure is God. And that's where I place my faith and my hope. That's where I stand.

A shift, a turn, a change unknown, a new path ahead, yet I walk alone. The diagnosis lands, a weight to bear, but in my heart, I know God is there. A journey starts anew, with fears in sight, but I won't surrender without a fight. Through every storm, through every tear, I'll face each challenge, knowing God is near.

This new chapter calls with lessons to learn, but through each twist I will discern that though the road may seem unclear, I walk by faith and have no fear. A shift in the journey, a new phase begun, I embrace the change with strength from the Son.

Though the road is hard and the night is long, in His grace, I find where I belong. For every diagnosis, a lesson to see, I'll rise with hope and live faithfully. Through every shift, I know I'll grow; with God by my side, I'll always glow.

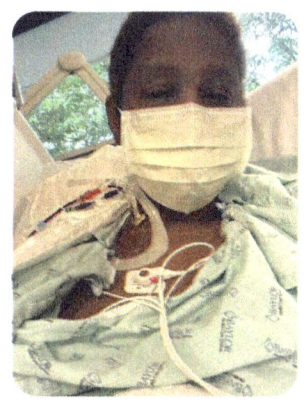

Oby Strong

CHAPTER 8

THE WEIGHT OF TRUTH AND THE JOURNEY WITHIN

FAMILY

John 8:32 KJV

"And ye shall know the truth, and the truth shall make you free."

Growing up as the third oldest of ten children, not counting the other siblings from my mom's husband, life was a mixture of chaos and connection. At times, being surrounded by so many siblings was refreshing, a source of comfort. Other times, it was overwhelming and confusing. After my mom passed away, I realized how important it was to stay connected to family, even though it wasn't always easy. Life has a way of shifting, revealing truths that we may not have been ready to face.

When I was diagnosed with breast cancer, it became painfully clear that life was changing rapidly, and the people I once called family had seemingly forsaken me. There were moments during my illness when I longed for the presence of my siblings. I yearned for conversations with my brothers, for meaningful exchanges with my sisters. But each attempt to connect seemed to lead only to more hurt and more pain. I felt misunderstood regarding my pain, my journey, and even my existence seemed invisible to them.

In the midst of this, I had to make the difficult decision to step away, to carve out a space for peace and rediscover my sense of self. It was a painful realization to accept that I had grown up in a world that often felt foreign to me, a world where the support I longed for was absent.

I never imagined my life would unfold this way, without the presence of parents, grandparents, or the close bond of siblings. I never thought this would be my story. But here I am, navigating the unexpected and finding my way through the emptiness.

The tears I shed day after day, week after week, and month after month, aching for someone, anyone besides my children, to understand the weight of what I'm carrying, began to take a toll on my health. It felt like I was drowning in sorrow and isolation, and yet, I had to find a way to push it aside.

Each diagnosis has brought with it a flood of memories and feelings of being unloved as a child. Every new pain has stirred the longing to have one more conversation with my mother, yet she's no longer here. As I face even more trials now, I can't help but wonder how things might have been different if I had been told the truth as an adult. I feel as if nobody truly loved me; nobody cared enough to protect the child I was.

I don't know what transpired between my biological parents, and I never felt it was my place to judge, so I never took that burden on. What I did take on, however, was the belief that my mother, my protector, was supposed to love me, guide me, and be honest with me and I never got that. I don't know how to express this pain, except to say exactly what I feel: something was missing in my childhood.

I've always felt different from my siblings, always felt like there was something I couldn't quite grasp, but I pushed through it. I pushed through as a child, as a teenager, and as an adult. Now, in the midst of all the chaos, I am being forced to face it and it hurts like hell.

The way I was raised knowing God, attending church regularly, praying constantly, and being taught to always tell the truth, believing that honesty would keep me safe shaped my childhood. I believed that my parents were my first line of defense. Now, as an adult, I find myself rethinking everything I was taught, questioning every decision my mother made. As I face this painful journey, the mental, emotional, and physical strain is overwhelming, and I am constantly searching for ways to cope.

This is the hardest part of my journey the unknown. Finding my biological father was a challenge, but I succeeded. Discovering the family on his side felt like a revelation. ,

Living with Lynch Syndrome and battling this autoimmune disorder called Cerebral Ataxia has been difficult, with unexpected symptoms of PML, GAD65, and white matter of the brain as challenges constantly emerging in my body. The chemotherapy and medications are taking a toll, making my mind race in circles. Some days I'm depressed, other days I'm happy; some moments I feel lonely, other times I crave solitude;

sometimes I feel peace, and other times I don't. It's a constant battle of emotions.

Yet, in the midst of it all, I am challenged to praise God; I am challenged to wake up every morning and say, "Lord, I thank You." It's a challenge, but I do it. Even in my pain, I have made it a priority to encourage others because in lifting others up, I also lift myself. I am grateful for God's love, and though I don't yet understand the reasons behind my trials, I trust that there is a purpose. And I hold on to the belief that, in time, I will understand why this is happening.

I had to forgive my mother, not because it was easy, but because God's grace has shown me mercy time and again. I am not perfect, far from it, and in His wisdom, God reminded me of my own imperfections. In my hurt, I learned to release the weight of my pain, to digress from the spiral of resentment, and to surrender myself to the fullness of humanity's flaws. Through forgiveness, I found a strange but beautiful peace, a quiet place where my feelings of being unloved no longer had power.

Forgiveness became the key to my mental clarity, the foundation of my emotional healing. And in letting go of what I could not change, I found strength to move forward, not bitter, but free.

Forgiveness didn't come all at once. It came in fragments, in quiet moments of surrender when the hurt felt too heavy to hold. It came as I sat with my pain, realizing that carrying anger only deepened my wounds. At first, forgiveness felt impossible. How could I forgive what felt like abandonment? How could I release the hurt feeling of being unloved, unseen, and unprotected as a child? But then I realized forgiveness wasn't for her alone; it was for me. It was the bridge to healing my mind, the balm for the ache in my spirit. It was the only way to move forward without dragging the chains of yesterday into tomorrow.

One might ask, how do you simply forgive? Or how do you feel about your mother not telling you who your biological father was? The truth is, my feelings about it are often baffling, leaving me lost for words. There are moments when the weight of it all consumes me, and I struggle to find peace within myself to deal with the hurt. I try, day by day, not to let that situation define the rest of my life. I've done my best to put it to rest, to move forward, but it remains one of the hardest things I've ever faced.

People often say, God is a healer, or you have to forgive your mom and let it go. But I've learned that those words, as well-intentioned as they may be, are easier said than lived. Forgiveness, when paired with unanswered questions and a racing mind trying to piece together the how and why, is not a simple task. It's a process that requires patience and grace with myself.

I remind others who offer advice: you never know how you'd respond until you're standing in the shoes of someone living through it. Until you face the reality of carrying those emotions and unanswered questions, it's impossible to fully understand. My journey through this has been anything but simple, but I am determined to keep pressing.

After forgiving my mom, myself, and others, I felt a weight lifted from my shoulders, a release I didn't know I so desperately needed. But forgiveness isn't the end of the journey; it's the beginning. Now, I must sit with the truth, face it head-on, and walk this path with courage. It hasn't been easy, and I know it won't get any easier. Yet, with grace and God's unending mercy, I hold onto the promise that I'll make it. Through tears in my eyes and pain in my body, I'll keep moving forward. Even on the hardest days, when the burden feels heavy, I cling to the truth that God is with me. And because of His strength, I know no matter what I will make it.

Now, I feel lighter. Forgiveness didn't erase the scars, but it gave me peace in their place. It reminded me that love, even flawed love, is still love. And it showed me that healing begins not when we wait for apologies but when we give ourselves permission to let go.

The truth is, I need family. I need to feel that I'm not enduring this in vain. I've grown in so many ways through this journey, and I've come to truly understand the value of friendship, love, understanding, and peace. But at times, the weight of my reality presses down on me. It's my life, and I must live it. I have to keep moving, keep pushing, keep believing, and keep holding onto faith and hope. That's what sustains me during these trials.

I pray that none of my family and friends ever has to endure what I'm going through, because it's not easy; it's incredibly hard on the body, mind, and spirit. You have to have a made-up mind to keep going. So many people I started this journey with have decided they couldn't fight anymore. The chemo, the pain, and the constant challenges all became too much, and they let go.

But that's not where I stand today. I stand with determination, even when I feel weak, weary, or angry. I still want to fight. Though frustration and grief sometimes spill out onto others, I do my best not to let my pain become someone else's burden. I'm not one to throw a pity party or dwell in sorrow. Instead, I've made a vow to celebrate my life.

I've decided that from this day forward, I will celebrate my birthday every year. Some years in the past, I didn't have the means to do so, and I chose to focus on breast cancer awareness instead. But now, I've committed to honoring my life. In 2025, I plan to have a grand birthday party, a true celebration of survival, resilience, and joy. And I pray that the Lord will grant me the strength to see that day and many more.

The weight of truth is heavy, deep, a burden carried where shadows sleep.
A journey within, a road untold, where broken hearts and fears unfold.
In the silence, it whispers loud, through layers of doubt, beneath the cloud.
It calls to the soul; it shakes the core, telling of wounds we can't ignore.
Each step forward feels like a strain, a battle within, a quiet pain.
But through the struggle, we find our way, emerging stronger, day by day.
The truth we carry is not our own but part of a journey we've always known.
A journey of healing, of facing the light, of finding our strength, even in the night.
So, we walk with grace, though the path is steep, embracing the lessons that make us weep.
For through the weight of the truth we bear, we discover ourselves, strong and aware.

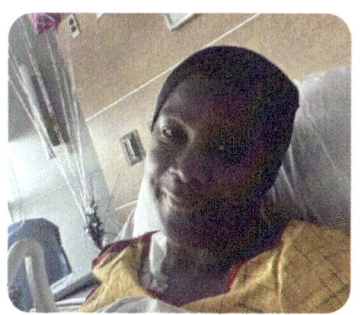

Oby Strong

CHAPTER 9

LIVING ON PURPOSE

GRACE AND GRATITUDE

2 Corinthians 12:9 KJV Grace

"And he said unto me, my grace is sufficient for thee: for my strength is made perfect in weakness. Most gladly therefore will I rather glory in my infirmities, that the power of Christ may rest upon me."

1 Thessalonians 5:18 KJV Gratitude

"In everything give thanks: for this is the will of God in Christ Jesus concerning you."

Ephesians 2:10 KJV Living with Purpose

"For we are his workmanship, created in Christ Jesus unto good works, which God hath before ordained that we should walk in them."

Through all of my triumphs and tribulations, I choose to live on purpose, anchored in grace and gratitude. Every challenge has shaped me, and every victory has strengthened me, reminding me of the beauty and resilience within. By embracing each day with intention, I honor the journey and the blessings that come with it.

Living on purpose, to me, means embracing every part of this journey even the painful, uncertain, and overwhelming parts. It means choosing to see the blessings in each day, no matter how small, and letting those moments remind me why I continue to fight. It's about finding meaning in each step, leaning on faith, and reaching out to lift others up even when my own struggles feel all-consuming.

Every day, I try to remind myself that I am here for a reason. That my story, though filled with hardship, might bring hope to someone else facing their own battles. I want to live intentionally, giving thanks to God for the strength He's given me and using whatever time I have to encourage others, to show compassion, and to create joy whenever I can.

I choose to live with purpose. I choose to fight this battle, even when it feels like everything in the medical book is being thrown at me. I choose to fight. I choose to win.

Still, there are times when I feel angry, frustrated, and overwhelmed. Times when the weight of it all threatens to crush me. But even in those moments of despair, I never not once thought about giving up. No matter how hard this battle has been, giving up has never been an option. My body grows tired. My mind grows weak, I get weary, I cry, I call friends, I scream, and I let it all out. But after I release it, I gather my strength and get back to the fight.

This battle is relentless, but so am I. Until my body decides it can no longer go on, I will keep fighting. I will never stop; I will never give up. This is my choice, my purpose, my life and I will face it head-on, every single day.

Living on purpose is finding peace, even in the storm, and allowing my faith to keep me grounded. It's a commitment to keep going, not just for myself, but for those who love me and for anyone who may be inspired by my journey.

When chemo started, I had to find faith. It wasn't something that came easily, but it was the anchor I needed to hold on to in the storm. As my body underwent transformation and faced the toll of treatment, I was forced to dig deeper to reach into the very core of who I was and trust God had a plan for me, even when I couldn't see it.

When my hair started to fall out, I felt a deep sense of loss. It was more than just hair it was a reminder of everything in my body, everything that was out of my control. I wanted to give up, to let the weight of it all pull me down. But in those moments of despair, I realized that this was just one chapter in my journey. My hair would grow back, and in the grand scheme of things, it was a temporary part of the story. What mattered more was the strength of my spirit and the resilience I was building through each challenge.

It was in those quiet, painful moments that I discovered the deeper purpose of life. I realized that what I was going through wasn't meant to break me but to shape me. Each trial, each struggle, was forging a fighter inside of me. I wasn't just enduring; I was fighting for my life. I was finding my strength in the most unexpected places, learning that true beauty wasn't in the things that could be lost but in the fire that burns within me to keep going.

My faith needed to stand strong, and I needed to trust that everything I was experiencing was part of the journey that would ultimately lead me to healing. It was a test, not just of my body, but of my spirit. And in the end, I realized that the fight wasn't just about surviving. it was about thriving through the storm, knowing that with faith, even the hardest days would lead to something better.

I asked God to rewrite my story; I needed Him to take the broken pieces of my life and somehow make them whole again. I didn't know how this journey would unfold, but I trusted that He could do what I couldn't bring redemption, healing, and purpose from the pain.

It was during one of these quiet moments of surrender that I came across a song by Donald Lawrence called "Rewritten." The lyrics, powerful and simple, resonated deeply within me. As I listened to the song, I felt my heart stir. The words were a reminder that God was not finished with me yet. He was rewriting my story, turning pages of my life in a way that only He could.

The chorus of the song spoke to me in a way I couldn't ignore. It felt like God was saying, "This chapter is not the end; it is just the beginning." His promise to rewrite my story wasn't just about the physical healing but about spiritual renewal. The more I meditated on the words, the more I understood. The song wasn't just about me surviving cancer; it was about me thriving in the process of becoming who God had always intended for me to be.

As my brain, my walk, and my body began to heal, I realized that this was more than a physical fight it was a spiritual one. And in the midst of it, I had been given a choice: to dwell in fear and despair or to create a space of peace, joy, and love.

I chose to create a space where the noise of the world, the overwhelming thoughts, and the constant worry could no longer invade. I decided to clear that space for God to work in me and through me. I knew that the only way to survive this journey was to lean into His presence and allow Him to fill every corner of my heart with love, patience, and grace. I also realized that as I began to fill that space with peace, I was also making room to love on others in a way I had never done before.

It became clear to me that this battle wasn't just for me; it was about how I could use my story to encourage others. Along this journey, I've come to realize that sometimes the smallest blessings carry the greatest weight. In the midst of pain, uncertainty, and countless setbacks, these small moments of grace have been like lifelines, anchoring me and reminding me of the good that still exists.

A small blessing might be a warm cup of tea on a difficult morning, the quiet comfort of a loved one's hand holding mine, or the sunlight streaming through my window just when I need it. It's the feeling of relief after a doctor's visit that went a little better than expected or the laughter that sneaks out in moments when I'd almost forgotten how to smile.

There are days when someone's kind words or a reassuring smile from a stranger lightens my load, reminding me that I'm not alone in this journey. My family, my friends, and even the nurses and doctors who show compassion all of them are small blessings weaving strength into my days. Each prayer offered, each card received, each gentle hug or phone call lifts me up in ways I could never have imagined.

In the quietest moments, I've also found blessings in my own strength and resilience qualities that I didn't fully realize were there until they were tested. The ability to keep going, to hold on to hope, even when the path is uncertain these are the blessings I carry with me, a constant reminder of the grace that exists within me.

These small blessings don't erase the struggle, but they make it bearable. They bring a glimmer of light to dark days, showing me that even in the hardest times, life offers moments of beauty and connection. And so, I hold onto these blessings, one by one. Finding strength and comfort in their presence.

Each morning, I wake up, which is a blessing in itself a chance to begin again, to take another step forward. In the simplest of moments, I find gratitude: the quiet morning light, the rhythm of my breath, the stillness before the day begins.

Being able to open my eyes, to see the world, to feel the start of a new day these are blessings I never take for granted.

I've learned to embrace these small blessings as pieces of hope. The ability to smile, even when my body is weary, even when the path ahead is daunting, is a gift that sustains me. A smile feels like a reminder of resilience, faith, and a little moment of peace that says, I am still here. It's a blessing I can offer to myself and to those around me, a way of sharing joy in the midst of struggle.

During my birthday month and the holidays, I often feel a wave of anxiety. These are times when I used to be busy cooking, celebrating, and enjoying family, but now they've become some of the hardest moments. The absence of my grandparents and parents feels overwhelming, and their loss is especially heavy during these times. But grief doesn't only show up on special occasions it's something I face daily. It's not just the grief of losing loved ones but also the grief of my changing health.

God continues to give me strength, helping me push forward through the pain. I'm holding on, pushing past the challenges, and trusting Him to carry me through.

Small blessings are put together to create something powerful: a thread of gratitude, a spark of light, and a quiet, steady courage that keeps me moving forward. Whatever you do, live on purpose.

There were times I stumbled, times I fell short, when my choices were far from right, and my heart was heavy with regret. But even then, God's mercy stood firm, shielding me from the consequences I truly earned. He didn't repay me with what my sins deserved; instead, He covered me in grace, wrapped me in love, and gave me chance after chance to rise again. I've seen His hand pull me from the depths, not because I was worthy, but because He is good.

Every blessing I hold, every breath I take, is a reminder that His plan is greater than my mistakes. Through trials, through tears, and through the moments of doubt, I've learned to trust that God's grace is what life is all about.

If I were to leave this world today, my greatest accomplishment would undoubtedly be my children. They are my legacy, my heart, and my strength, the reason I continue to fight through every trial. I am deeply grateful for the blessing of being married twice and for guiding me through this life.

Looking back, I've lived my life with a smile, even in the face of pain. No, I'm not perfect, but I've embraced this journey with faith and gratitude. For every high and low, for every moment of joy and struggle, I can only say, Lord, I thank You.

I wake each day with strength anew to face the trials life leads me through.
With courage bound and spirit high, I lift my head toward the sky.
The journey twists, the road may bend, yet with each step, I find a friend.
In faith, in hope, in love so true, in purpose clear, my life made new.
Though storms may come and shadows fall, I walk with grace; I stand up tall.
For every breath, a reason is found to cherish life on holy ground.
In purpose rooted deep and strong, I choose to live, to sing my song.
For no defeat, no loss, or pain can dim the light my soul has gained.
So here I stand, steadfast and free, living on purpose, boldly, with faith as my guide, my path to see, each step a gift, my destiny.

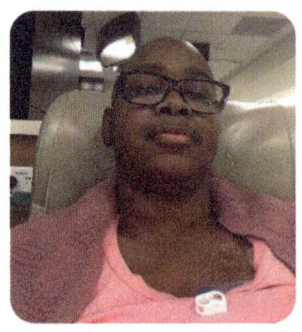

Oby Strong

CHAPTER 10

FAITH IN THE FIRE

LIVING AS A CHRISTIAN THROUGH LIFE'S TRIALS

1 Peter 1:7 KJV

"That the trial of your faith, being much more precious than of gold that perisheth, though it be tried with fire, might be found unto praise and honor and glory at the appearing of Jesus Christ."

Poem by: Carol Wimmer

When I say, "I am a Christian," I'm not shouting, "I've been saved!" I'm whispering, "I get lost sometimes; that's why I chose this way." When I say, "I am a Christian," I don't speak with human pride; I'm confessing that I stumble, needing God to be my guide. When I say, "I am a Christian," I'm professing that I'm weak and pray for strength to carry on. When I say, "I am a Christian," I'm not bragging of success; I'm admitting that I've failed and can never pay the debt. When I say, "I am a Christian," I don't think I know it all; I submit to my confusion, asking humbly to be taught. When I say, "I am a Christian," I'm not claiming to be perfect; my flaws are far too visible, but God believes I'm worth it. When I say, "I am a Christian," I still feel the sting of pain. I have my share of heartache, which is why I seek God's name. When I say, "I am a Christian," I do not wish to judge; I have no authority; I only know I'm loved.

One of the things people don't often talk about when we're sick, especially as Christians, is that we, too, feel pain. We hurt, we have doubts, and we question. It's easy for others to assume that because we have faith, we should always be strong and never show our vulnerability. But the truth is, being a Christian doesn't mean we are immune to suffering or that we don't experience the emotional weight of illness. We're human, and we feel the depth of pain, confusion, and fear just like anyone else.

What sets us apart is not that we don't hurt, but that we know God is there, even in the midst of it all. We know that, despite our doubts, He is still faithful. It's not about having all the answers or never feeling overwhelmed, but it's about how we navigate those moments of darkness. How do we pull ourselves out of despair and depression? How do we trust God when everything seems uncertain?

As Christians, we often face not only our own struggles but also the expectations of others the pressure to appear strong, to "be the example," and to act as if our faith should always keep us from feeling weak. But the reality is trusting God doesn't mean we don't experience hardship or that we don't have moments where we question everything. It's about knowing where our true strength comes from.

Throughout my journey with cancer and the many challenges that have followed whether it's dealing with my health, learning about my biological father, or facing unexpected obstacles I've felt a range of emotions. Hurt, anger, confusion. But I've come to realize that none of those feelings take away from my spiritual beliefs. In fact, they prove that I'm human.

There have been times when I've lashed out, when the weight of everything was too much, but in those moments, I've learned that God isn't distant. He wants us to trust Him, especially in our vulnerability. He wants us to come to Him with our anger, our pain, and our questions. It's in those raw, unguarded moments that we are invited to cry out for forgiveness and seek His answers, even when we don't fully understand what's happening.

I firmly believe that my heart, though broken at times, is valid. My pain is real, and I don't dismiss it. I'm not saying that I have it all figured out far from it. What I'm saying is that in my imperfections, God is still at work. He takes what's broken and creates something new. My journey, with all its struggles and flaws, is a testimony to His grace. And even though I've had moments of doubt, I believe that in those very struggles, God is making me into something greater than I could have ever imagined.

Being sick and a Christian is one of the most challenging things I've had to experience. There's a unique weight that comes with battling a life-threatening illness while holding onto your faith. People often assume that because you're a Christian, you should always be strong, unwavering, and full of hope. Sickness tests everything. It tests your body, your strength, and your faith.

There are days when you feel completely broken, when you wonder why this is happening or how you'll make it through another round of treatment or bad news. You wrestle with questions like "Where is God in this? Why me? What purpose could this possibly serve?" These are not easy questions, and having faith doesn't always make them disappear.

The hardest part is balancing the human side of suffering with the spiritual side of trust. There's a part of you that wants to scream, cry, and be angry. And then there's the part of you that knows you're called to lean on God, to trust that He is in control even when everything feels out of control. It's a delicate dance between holding onto hope and acknowledging the very real, very heavy pain you're carrying.

But what I've learned is that faith doesn't mean being free from fear, doubt, or pain. It means trusting God in spite of those things. It means bringing your brokenness to Him, knowing that He can handle your tears, your questions, and even your anger. It means realizing that He is present in the darkness, even when you can't see Him.

Being sick and a Christian force you to confront your humanity while clinging to your divinity in Christ. It's not about being perfect or having all the answers it's about surrendering, even when it feels impossible. It's about finding moments of grace in the struggle and trusting that, somehow, God is working even in the pain. And while it's one of the hardest things, it's also one of the most deeply transformative experiences of faith.

The Bible verse that says, "Faith is the substance of things hoped for, the evidence of things not seen" (Hebrews 11:1) perfectly captures the heart of my journey. It brings clarity to everything I've been through and gives me hope as I continue to move forward. This verse reminds me that faith isn't about having all the answers or seeing the full picture it's about trusting in what I can't yet see, believing that God is working in ways I don't fully understand.

My journey has been filled with moments of uncertainty times when I didn't know what was coming next or how I would make it through. Yet, this verse reassures me that even when I can't see the outcome, my faith is a foundation I can stand on. It's not about understanding everything in the moment but trusting that every step, every decision, and even every hardship has a purpose in God's great plan.

Faith gives me the strength to keep going, even when the road feels long and the challenges seem overwhelming. It reminds me that the way I'm carrying myself and the way I'm choosing to trust in God's promises are all part of something bigger. Even when I don't fully understand what's happening, I know it's all working together for my good and His glory.

I would encourage people to approach others with compassion rather than judgment and to extend grace just as we would hope to receive it ourselves. When someone is sick or overwhelmed by the weight of life's challenges, it's easy for anger, frustration, or fear to take hold. In those moments, they may say or do things that don't reflect who they are at their core or align with their faith. But that doesn't mean they're beyond grace.

Faith in the fire was the moment I realized my life was burning up around me everything felt chaotic and out of control, and my faith was being tested like never before. It was a pivotal moment where I knew I had to reconcile the two: the flames of my struggles and the foundation of my faith. Somehow, I had to find a way to walk through this fire, leaning into my faith to guide me, sustain me, and carry me forward.

It wasn't easy. There were days when I questioned everything, days when the weight of the journey felt too heavy to bear. But looking back, I realize that God had been preparing me for this season long before I arrived here. My time spent studying the word, understanding my spirituality, and deepening my relationship with Him became my anchor when the storms hit. Those seeds of faith planted years ago began to grow in the midst of the fire, giving me strength to keep going.

This journey has been anything but easy, and the fire has refined me in ways I never imagined. But here I am, still standing, still journeying, and still trusting. Faith in the fire isn't about avoiding the flames; it's about walking through them, knowing that God is with you every step of the way. It's about letting the fire burn away what no longer serves you and finding the strength, courage, and hope to keep moving forward.

The journey of faith has become so much more than just a part of who I am it's shaping how I live, how I face challenges, and how I find meaning in this life. I'm learning to navigate my world differently, to approach life with more grace for myself, and to embrace the idea that living well isn't about perfection. It's about growing, adapting, and accepting that failure, sadness, and tears are all part of being human.

Pain is universal; it's not exclusive to or separate from faith it's a part of our experience. When we strip everything back, pain and sickness are raw realities of life that don't care about labels or belief systems. These struggles demand to be felt and faced. They don't make you less faithful or less strong; they make you human.

It's okay to feel broken, to not have it all figured out, and to admit that life is hard. That's not a lack of faith, it's the reality of living in a world where suffering exists. And while faith can bring comfort, strength, and hope, it doesn't erase the very real emotions that come with sickness and hardship. That's why we need to talk about it openly. Not everything has to be tied up in neat answers, because life isn't straightforward.

What I've come to realize is that faith isn't about avoiding the hard parts of life, it's about finding God in the midst of them. It's about holding onto hope while being honest about the pain. And it's about reminding ourselves that feeling sadness, anger, or frustration doesn't mean we've failed. It means we're alive. It means we're living through the fire, and that is an act of courage.

It's important to remember that we all fall short at times, and sickness or hardship can amplify emotions we're struggling to control. Instead of judging or criticizing, we should offer understanding, patience, and kindness. Grace and mercy are gifts that we've been freely given by God, and we're called to extend the same to others.

Prayer is also a powerful tool, it changes hearts, minds, and situations. When we choose to pray for the sick or those who are struggling, we're inviting God to work in ways we can't. It's through His goodness that transformation happens, not just in the person we're praying for but also in ourselves. Encouragement, grace, and prayer are how we reflect God's love and remind others that they're not alone, no matter how dark or difficult their journey may be.

So, let's move with love and humility, trusting in God's goodness and allowing His mercy to flow through us to others. It's in these small acts of grace that we bring light to even the darkest places.

The flames rise high, the heat intense, life's trials pressing without defense.
Yet through the blaze, I choose to stand, held secure by His mighty hand.
The fire defines; it burns away the fears that threaten to lead astray.
It shapes my soul; it tests my might, turning darkness into light.
Though tears may fall and strength may wane, His promises steady me through the pain.
For in the fire, my faith grows strong, a reminder that His love leads me on.
I won't be consumed; I won't despair, for God's presence meets me everywhere.
The flames may roar, but they cannot stay; faith in the fire shows me the way.

Oby Strong

Acknowledgements

John 15:12-13, KJV

"This is my commandment, that ye love one another, as I have loved you. Greater love hath no man than this, that a man lay down his life for his friends."

Thank you, Lord, for the strength you have poured into me for the gift of each day. Thank you for walking with me, even when the path seemed unbearable, and for holding me when I felt too weak to go on. I am grateful for your unending love and grace, which has surrounded me through every battle, every victory, and every setback. You have placed incredible people in my life, and I know this is your love in action. Thank you, Lord, for the blessings, the courage, and the will to keep fighting. I give you all the praise, all the honor, and all my love.

I would like to acknowledge the countless individuals who have walked with me through this journey, lifting me up in ways that I will never forget.

I will begin with my children, Desmond, Demond, and Jemesha; your love has been the foundation that carried me through each day. Thank you for being my motivation, my joy, and my reason to keep smiling and fighting. Every smile and every hug from you has meant the world to me, grounding me in hope and love.

Thank you, Kelby, for always supporting me on this journey. Your understanding of the importance of family, relationships, and forgiveness means so much. As siblings, we may have our moments of disagreement but love always brings us back together. Your kindness and presence are truly appreciated. Thank you again!

To my dear friend Karen: Thank you for opening your home and heart to me. You cared for me when I was at my most vulnerable, guiding me through chemo and all other challenges that came along. Your selflessness, love, and unwavering support gave me a safe place to heal. I can never repay you for all you've done, but I am deeply, endlessly grateful.

To my church family: It has been your prayers that lifted me up and gave me strength when my faith felt thin. Knowing that so many hearts were praying for me brought me a sense of peace and courage. Thank you for standing with me, for believing in miracles, and for reminding me that I am never alone.

To my blood-related family: Each of you has been a gift, a blessing, and a source of strength. I am grateful to walk this journey with you by my side, and I am forever changed by the love and kindness you have shown me. Thank you from the depths of my heart.

To Ingrid Edwards and Anthony White: Thank you for always being my rock. You have been there to lift me up, to see me through every twist and turn, and to pull me out of my darkest days. Thank you for taking me where I needed to go, for listening when I needed to talk, and for crying with me when words weren't enough. You have been a constant source of strength, and I am so blessed to call you both a friend.

To Charlotte Mullins and Melissa Chapple: I am grateful for your unwavering love, prayers, and kindness, which have been a comfort beyond measure. Knowing you were by my side, praying and sending me strength, has meant everything to me. Thank you for your gratitude and for your gentle presence during the hardest days.

To my Wilmer Hutchins alumni: Thank you for the encouragement, the check-ins, and the unending kindness. You have shown me that community runs deep, that I am part of something greater. Your support has been a constant reminder that I am held and supported by a family that extends beyond blood.

To Freda Bates and Aaron Sherman: Thank you for your selfless care and support. You picked me up when I couldn't do it myself, helped me keep my home in order, and made sure I was never alone. Thank you for taking me to bingo and for the laughter and light you brought with you. Your visits brought me joy and helped me feel connected to the world outside my home. I appreciate you more than words can express.

Thank you to the American Cancer Society and to every person I've been blessed to meet through this remarkable organization. Your support has been a vital part of my journey, lifting me up when I needed it most. Each walk, each event, and each interaction has given me strength and reminded me of the incredible community that surrounds me.

It is with a heart full of love and deep gratitude that I acknowledge my beloved Uncle Eurn Bluitt Jr. Though words can never fully express the depth of my appreciation, I want to honor the unwavering love, guidance, and support he offered me from childhood to adulthood. Uncle Jr., you were always there, standing by me through every storm and every joy. Your strength, resilience, and love have been a constant throughout my life. Even in your own times of struggle, you never hesitated to show me the way with kindness and understanding. You never changed, and I will always remember the peace and comfort you brought to my life. You were my pillar, my protector, and my favorite uncle. As you rest now, know that your memory, your spirit, and your love will live on in my heart. You were a blessing, Uncle Jr., and I will carry your legacy with me always. May your soul rest in eternal peace. I love you deeply. Thank you for everything. Your Chicken

Reather McCowin, Veta Jackson, Carol Jennings, Janice Reason, Dolores Washington, and the entire Triumph family, thank you for your unending prayers and for lifting me up with all your cares. I appreciate you for keeping me grounded, rooted in grace, and for loving me every day. You took me in as one of your own, and for this I am forever grateful. I may not have called or texted each day, but I felt your love guiding my way. Your grace has helped me stand, a gift from God, through a faithful hand. My heart is grateful, more than words can say.

To my Metaverse family: Thank you, Skotta2Shotta, Willie Beaman, Kingvr, MsWms, Jaywillvr, Burdenofproof, Queenscorpio, OnyxShae, Legacy (Queen), Hitmanvr, Semi_Colon, Ponay, Beau Fowler, Saxion, Zuly, Aquarius, Seekavr, PJazzy, and Jojo. Through the digital world, your kindness, strength, and compassion have lifted me up, helping me face challenges with courage and hope. Thank you for being part of this journey and for giving me a sense of community and support. I am grateful for every moment, every laugh, and every word shared.

Thank you to my Facebook friends and family for your constant support, your prayers, and the love you've shown me through each step of this journey. Your kind words, messages, and encouragement have lifted my spirits on days when I've needed it most. Thank you for being there, for reaching out, and for reminding me that I'm never alone in this fight. Your presence means more than words can say. Thank you.

My Oby family: Tresa Bruner, Jerome Oby, Taryn Hill, Damian Oby, Michael Cooper, Toni Douglas, and the entire Oby family. Where do I begin? There is so much to be said. When I felt like giving up, you were the ones who kept me going. You showed me love without me even asking for it. It was a love I could feel, even from afar, and for that, I am deeply grateful. You lift me up in ways I can't fully describe. You never let me fall, never let me go. Your prayers are filled with power, your love overflowing with grace. You've held me close when I needed it the most, and for that, I will always appreciate you. My family, my strength, my heart, thank you for being a part of this journey with me. You are more than a blessing; you are my anchor.

Angela James: Thank you, girl, for looking out for me when I needed someone the most. When I needed a steady praying hand, someone to stand by me, you were right there. I could call you during the late midnight hour, and without hesitation you'd be there to listen. I am grateful to have you in my life.

My bingo family: Marilyn Scott, Clarice Jones, and the Balch Springs bingo family, thank you ladies and gentlemen for all the love and care you've shown me. For calling to check on me, for sending me your light, and for lifting me up with your prayers. The bingo outings meant so much to me, those moments of laughter and connection. You stood by me when my mother passed, offering me comfort when I needed comforting. You didn't just talk about what I was going through but focused on what I'm getting through. That made all the difference. I love you all for that. You've been a true blessing in my life.

THE GALLERY OF LOVE

"My Sunshine"

"My Kelly and Beyonce"
During the depths of my sickness, these two little stars, Leelee and Nova,
Brought me so much joy.
With their pretty wigs and full of joy and laughter and love when I needed it most.
Being "Aunt Sheena" to them is a role I cherish deeply.
Thank you, Leelee and Nova,
For loving on me and lifting my spirits in ways you'll never fully know.
My Sunshine!

In quiet moments and storms that rage, you stood beside me, page by page.
With open heart, in silence shared, you lifted burdens, showed you cared.
Through laughter bright, and shadow deep, you held my hand when I couldn't sleep.
With every smile, each kind embrace, you brought me love, you gave me grace.
So, here's my thanks, in words so small, for standing strong, for giving your all.
In friendship's light, I see anew, the beauty found in friends like you.

Made in the USA
Coppell, TX
29 September 2025

60632017R10056